Journey through

SAXONY-ANHALT

Photos by
Tina and Horst Herzig

Text by
Ernst-Otto Luthardt

Stürtz

Hasseröder
Hasseröder
Ratskeller

Hotel
Gothisches Haus

First page:
In 1883, on the 400th anniversary of Martin Luther's birthday, this monument was unveiled in Eisleben, his place of birth. One of the reliefs on the base depicts him translating the Bible at Wartburg Castle.

Previous page:
The town hall in Wernigerode is one of the most beautiful and most famous in Germany. It was first mentioned as a casino and court in 1277. The half-timbered storey was added at the end of the 15th century. The building took on its present appearance following a fire in the middle of the 16th century.

Below:
"It is like wandering through a fairytale one is being told and has all the character of the Elysian

fields", enthused Goethe in a letter to Frau von Stein of the Garden Kingdom of Dessau-Wörlitz. Here the Flora Temple.

Page 10/11: *View from the castle of Stolberg. The old official residence of the counts of Stolberg, first mentioned at the beginning of the 13th century, was originally a mining settlement. Otto zu Stolberg-Wernigerode was vice-chancellor of the German Empire under Bismarck.*

Contents

The market square in Wittenberg. The statue of Luther unveiled in 1821 was designed by Johann Gottfried Schadow and Karl Friedrich Schinkel. On the left is the town hall erected in the style of the Renaissance, with the towers of the city church of St Mary's in the background on the right.

Contrary to popular belief, the German federal state of Saxony-Anhalt was not first created in 1990 when the Berlin Wall came down. Pieced together in the aftermath of the Second World War in 1947 from the province of Saxony, the country of Anhalt, bits of Thuringia and two tiny enclaves belonging to Brunswick, when the Iron Curtain clanged shut in 1952 the province of Saxony-Anhalt was split into the East German districts of Halle and Magdeburg. While the province of Saxony was the result of haggling over territory at the Congress of Vienna in 1814/15, in which the Prussians laid claim to the northern part of the kingdom of Saxony and merged it with older estates, such as Eichsfeld and Magdeburg, the history of the Anhalt part of Saxony-Anhalt goes back much further.

The first Ascanian to call himself count of Anhalt was Heinrich, grandson of the legendary Count Albrecht the Bear. This was in 1212. His successors then outdid each other in the division of the county into ever tinier states and estates, the most idiosyncratic example being Plötzkau, which consisted of a castle and a few huts. It nevertheless maintained an army of 20 men – which neither made it a state nor proved effective in scaring off potential potentates. Later on Prince Joachim Ernst (1536–1586) managed to unite Anhalt's various dominions under his singular rule, only for them to go their separate ways on his death. All that remained were Anhalt-Köthen, Anhalt-Bernburg and Anhalt-Dessau which in the mid 19th century, after the first two lines had died out, merged to form the duchy of Anhalt. In 1918 this became a free state.

Some of its princes wrote history. One was Ludwig of Anhalt-Köthen (1579–1650), cofounder and patron of the *Fruchtbringende Gesellschaft* or Fruitbearing Society who made it their job to free the disrespected and neglected German language "from the alien, oppressive yoke of languages" that had made German "watery and too salty / Through the splendour of foreign

words" and set it "upon the most glorious throne of honour". There was also Imperial General Field Marshal Leopold I of Anhalt-Dessau (1676–1747) who taught the Prussians to march in step and introduced the iron ramrod for muskets. The Old Dessauer, as he was known, was at home on the battle field and extremely well-liked. A popular march tune keeps his memory alive.
On September 1, 1745, Christian August of Anhalt-Zerbst married his sixteen-year-old daughter Sophie to Peter, duke of Holstein, who had been adopted by Empress Elizabeth of Russia and succeeded her on the throne. He only had six months to enjoy his life as emperor, however. At her wedding, Sophie (now called Katharina) vowed to "please her husband, Elizabeth and the Russian people" and "to do everything to achieve this". The bit about pleasing her husband wasn't quite true; Sophie/Katharina decided to get rid of the infantile Peter as fast as possible and seize the throne for herself.

The bird-catcher: King Heinrich I

When Heinrich I heard the news that he had been elected king of Germany, he is said to have been indulging in his favourite pastime of bird-catching. This was in 919 near his imperial palace of Quitilingaburg. His alleged forest of finches has long disappeared and is now the town of Quedlinburg. The many visitors who stroll along the UNESCO-patronised streets lined with splendid half-timbered buildings like to believe the rhyme that claims Heinrich was out hunting when made regent (*Herr Heinrich sitzt am Vogelherd*) – whether true or not. A more historically sound place to meet the monarch and his wife is the Romanesque abbey church of St Servatius, in whose crypt the royal tombs are preserved. Although fairly ancient itself, the aisled basilica from 1129 is the fourth place of worship to be erected on this site.
On Schlossberg, also in Quedlinburg, is the house where Friedrich Gottlieb Klopstock first saw the light of day in 1724. The poet was more popular during his lifetime than many writers before or after him. When he died in Hamburg in 1803, tens of thousands joined the funeral cortege. Colleague Gotthold Ephraim Lessing preferred to look ahead and wrote a four-liner in which he predicted the literary fate of the deceased:

"Who will not praise Klopstock?
But will everyone read him? – No.
We wish to be less extolled
And read with more diligence."

It's not far from Klopstock's former house to the market square where a statue of Roland bearing a sword stands guard outside the town hall. About one third of the Rolands still in Germany can be found in Saxony-Anhalt. As opposed to the giant in Stendal, who's over five metres (16 feet) tall, Quedlinburg's Roland is a mere dwarf at just two-and-three-quarters of a metre (nine feet). In 1477 he was removed from his plinth and only returned four hundred years later. Maybe this is why he looks so grim. Or maybe it's because he's gone deaf from the loud chimes of the market church bells.

The prominent figures of Magdeburg

The famous stone knight on the marketplace in the Saxony-Anhalt's capital of Magdeburg has been here since the middle of the 13th century. The monument from the Romanesque period – the original was replaced by a copy in 1966 and is now in the city's museum of cultural history – probably depicts Emperor Otto I who made the Carolingian centre of trade on the River Elbe his official seat and thus the hub of the empire. This was no coincidence; the move was carefully calculated, as Otto had set his sights on the nearby land of the Slavs. To this end the emperor founded Moritz Monastery in 937, whom he gave the right to hold markets, mint coins and levy tolls in 965. Three years later the archbishopric of Magdeburg was established, conceived as the organisational and ideological control post for Germany's expansion to the east.

When the monastic church, which had since been made a cathedral, was consumed by fire in 1207, construction very soon started on a replacement house of God. The cathedral of St Mauritius and St Katharina, consecrated in 1363 and the first Gothic cathedral on German soil, not only houses the final resting place of Otto I and his wife Editha but also a number of outstanding sculptures. Examples include the likenesses of the clever and foolish virgins from the mid 13th century and of the cathedral's two patron saints.

Missionaries, merchants and colonists gradually took the city's constitution eastwards. Magdeburg Rights became the most widely disseminated German town charter in the Middle Ages; towns that adopted it included Wrocław, Szczecin, Kraków and Lviv.

No less than two monuments in Magdeburg are dedicated to Otto von Guericke, or rather to the two hemispheres with which in the mid 17th century he spectacularly proved the existence of atmospheric pressure. The genius scientist and inventor, who was also mayor of Magdeburg and a distinguished diplomat,

Schloss Oranienbaum, seen here with the main courtyard, was begun in 1683 as a summer seat for Count Johann Georg II of Anhalt-Dessau's wife, a princess of Orange-Nassau. The plans were drawn up by Dutchman Cornelius Ryckwaert.

joined two half-circles measuring about 50 cm (20") in diameter and extracted the air from them using a piston pump he had developed himself. He then harnessed a team of 16 and one of 30 horses to the hemispheres and tried to get the animals to pull them apart. They didn't succeed.

Infinitely beautiful gardens

Like his famous grandfather before him, Old Dessauer Leopold I, Leopold Friedrich Franz III (1740–1817) was earmarked for a career in the military. He joined the Prussian army at the age of twelve but left when he was 18 due to a more pressing engagement: that of prince of Anhalt-Dessau. Determined to improve the economic and social conditions in his country, he began looking for liked-minded, progressive individuals. Fate was on his side; the young regent soon met Friedrich Wilhelm von Erdmannsdorff, just four years his senior, who supported the prince in his enlightened views. And these weren't merely words; Leopold III first showed that he practised what he preached when in order to pay off four million talers of war reparations he failed to burden his subjects with heavy taxes but instead sold off some of his personal effects to foot the bill. So that he could study the new doctrines of economy in what was then the most advanced country in this field, he and Erdmannsdorff twice travelled to England. The pair also went to France and Italy where they pursued their interests in ancient art and architecture.
Leopold III then began to reform his dominions. He set new standards in social services, healthcare, schooling and especially agriculture. Even Karl Marx had to admit that the principality was a "miniature model state". The prince also aimed to combine the practical with the aesthetic through specific design of the countryside, proving both visionary and pragmatic in his endeavours. While he devoted his energies to his natural surroundings, his no less ingenious friend Erdmannsdorff concentrated on the architecture. The two men's first undertaking was what's now known as the Garden Kingdom

of Dessau-Wörlitz. As the terrain was limited by the dyke along the Elbe, the park was relatively narrow and long, tracing the line of the river for some way. In time more and more areas were landscaped. As well as integrating older gardens, such as Oranienbaum and Mosigkau, new features were added, among them the Georgium and Luisium palaces, the woodland park on Sieglitzer Berg and Großkühnau Park. Johann Wolfgang von Goethe visited the gardens in 1778 and found them "infinitely beautiful". They inspired him to develop the park on the River Ilm in Weimar.

Salt city

Halle was granted market rights in c. 1000. The four salt springs in the meadows along the River Saale proved a gold mine, catapulting the city to power and prosperity. As a sign of their pride and confidence the citizens erected the Roter Turm or red tower in the middle of the marketplace in 1418. But then trouble struck. They began to quarrel and various factions formed. The man to profit from this was Archbishop Ernst III of Saxony; he conquered Halle in 1478 and decided at the meeting of parliament one year later to "build without delay a stronghold near or in Halle to better keep the city obedient, obsequious and quiet." The Moritzburg was finished in 1503 and is now an art museum containing paintings and graphics from the Middle Ages to the present day, including a large collection of Expressionist works.
The beginning of the new palace marked the end of old Castle Giebichenstein which gradually paled into insignificance. Of the many legends surrounding it the most famous is the one about the spectacular escape of Ludwig, count of Thuringia. He is said to have jumped from his dungeon in the castle 40 metres (130 feet) down into the River Saale, earning him the nickname The Leaper. Centuries later the Romantics discovered the ruins. "I have never seen the world more beautiful", Joseph von Eichendorff once gushed of Giebichenstein and its lush surroundings.
Halle was also the birthplace of great composer George Frideric Handel in 1685. He began studying law at the university and also playing the organ before he left town, seldom to return. Despite this, his memory has been kept very much alive at the first-class festival held here in his honour since 1922. One of the great ecclesiasts of Halle was also a great philanthropist. Towards the end of the 17th century practising Pietist August Hermann Francke was moved to turn the orphanage in his charge into an educational institution which with

As the name Teufelsmauer or Devil's Wall suggests, this bizarre riff between Ballenstedt in the south-east and Blankenburg in the northwest is said to have been created by the Evil One himself.

its schools, boarding school, printing works, bookshop and apothecary evolved into a tiny independent district in its own right. It has miraculously survived various epochs, rulers and political systems to this day.

Köthen and Johann Sebastian Bach

Including the palace chapel, the royal seat of Köthen once had four churches – but not a single organ. In this respect, the Reformed court was decidedly puritanical. When in 1717 Johann Sebastian Bach took up his post here he knew what the situation was – yet still placed his hopes in his new employer. Prince Leopold of Anhalt-Köthen was nine years younger than his 32-year-old *Hofkapellmeister* or royal master of music. His travels had introduced him to both Europe's famous collections of art and its grand concert halls. Leopold loved the Muses and music in particular. He also played the violin, harpsichord and viol.

When Bach returned from Carlsbad (now Karlovy Vary) with the prince in 1720, he found his children without a mother. His wife Maria Barbara had died during his absence. After taking a year and a half to find a new consort, he finally married Anna Magdalena Wilcke, a soprano at court and just 20 years old. She gave him 13 children; Bach adored her. In their second year of marriage he dedicated his *Notebook for Anna Magdalena Bach* to her and three years later a second. The absence of an organ in Köthen encouraged Bach's output of secular music; in 1721 he wrote his six famous *Brandenburg Concertos* for Margrave Christian Ludwig of Brandenburg. Johann Sebastian modestly referred to them as "six concerts avec plusieurs instruments" (six concertos for various instruments).

Bach and Prince Leopold both took wives in the same year. Princess Friederike Henriette of Anhalt-Bernburg, with her doll-like head, was one of the prince's Anhalt relations. The young magnate now had to divide his attentions between his new paramour and his music and his *Kapellmeister* was concerned. "It very much seems as if the musical inclination of the prince is on the wane", he complained to his

View out across the Elbe of the cathedral of St Mauritius and St Katharina in Magdeburg. The vast Gothic edifice was begun in 1209, two years after the previous Ottonian building had burned down.

friend Erdmann. And although the prince's lady love soon died, Bach was drawn to Leipzig. However, even after his departure he remained in contact with the "gracious prince who both knows and loves music".

Heaven on earth

Like Goethe's Mephistopheles, the two men who on July 4, 1999, found the Sky Disc on Mittelberg near Nebra were obviously "part of that power that always wants evil yet always creates good". They were grave robbers who wanted nothing else but to get as good a price as they could for the loot they had found; apart from the Sky Disc their metal detectors had unearthed swords, axes, armbands and a chisel. An antiques dealer from Cologne fobbed them off with DM 31,000 and sold the find on to someone else. Changing hands several times, the disc was eventually slipped to a couple of receivers of stolen goods for DM 300,000 who were out to make the deal of their lives but ended up falling flat on their faces. Instead of the alleged 'buyer' handing over the agreed sum of DM 700,000, the state archaeologist of Saxony-Anhalt handed the crooks over to the police. This was in a hotel in Basle in Switzerland in February 2002.
Once the criminals had been relieved of their goods, the scientists stepped in – and were completely amazed. The bronze disc, which is 32 cm or about a foot in diameter and weighs 2.3 kilograms (5 lb), turned out to be the oldest physical depiction of the sky in the history of humankind. The gold applications, which have been amended several times, are variously interpreted as the full moon (or possibly the sun), a crescent moon, the Seven Sisters, stars (25), horizontal arches for sunrise and sunset and a solar barge. There are many hypotheses as to the purpose of the disc. Some believe it to be a calendar charting the solar year (including instruments for calculating the date of the solstice), others a device for cult use and yet others an artefact of religious significance. Investigations as to the origin of the metals used also threw up a few surprises; the copper came from a mine near Salzburg in Austria yet the gold and tin are probably from Cornwall in

England. The original Sky Disc is on view at the museum of prehistory in Halle. Near the site where the disc was discovered there is now a multimedia visitors' centre named Arche Nebra which, since opening in 2007, has become a real attraction.

A sweet dream

Even if not invented in the Hanseatic town of Salzwedel in the Altmark, the layered cake or *Baumkuchen*, to give it its German name, was certainly perfected there. Or so say the locals. Success has proved them right. Packed in attractive tins, this delicious cake has not only invaded the tea tables of various European courts but also earned great acclaim further afield. And continues to do so. However, as with most indigenous products it tastes best enjoyed close to home – with either tea, coffee, wine or cognac. Or treated to a dose of advocaat, ice-cream and/or cream. It's important that you don't slice it from top to bottom like any ordinary cake but instead cut it into small, semicircular discs. Only then can you see its rings – like those that mark the age of a tree, hence the name *Baumkuchen* or tree cake.
Friederike Louise Lentz, the proprietress of the Neustädter Keller inn, not only provided the original recipe for Salzwedel's *Baumkuchen* but also took care of the marketing. When Friedrich Wilhelm IV visited Salzwedel on May 26, 1841, the aforementioned cake was served. After the monarch had happily eaten his fill of the sweet delicacy, he asked if he might take the rest home to his wife. Madame Lentz leapt at the opportunity to become a prospective royal supplier. At Christmas she sent the king another *Baumkuchen*, the popularity of which soon spread. It didn't take long before the courts in Vienna and St Petersburg also began placing their orders in Salzwedel.

From Heaven above

When Martin Luther hammered his *Ninety-Five Theses* against the selling of papal indulgences to the door of the Schlosskirche in Wittenberg, the consequences were vast, affecting not just the church but the whole of society. The tiny royal seat became the cradle of the Reformation, the origin of great change that swept throughout the entire world. It's thus no surprise that the Luther towns of Wittenberg and Eisleben, the places where Luther was born and died, are now on the UNESCO list of World Heritage Sites.
Luther knew very well that his loud "no" to the Roman Catholic church meant the establishment of a new, Protestant church where the form of the service was to take on a special significance.

The rocky core of the Brocken is around 300 million years old. Unlike the storm-weathered, largely barren summit the middle of the granite mountain is girded with forest.

In 1524 he thus sat down with his friends Johann Walter and Conrad Rupff for three weeks to compile a book of German hymns which were to become part of the liturgy. The three discussed, wrote music and penned lyrics, in part making use of well-known, secular melodies. Some familiar tunes appeared in new arrangements; folk melodies were given a new text.

Eleven years later Luther wrote a now famous tune for his children along the same lines. German-French theologian and organist Albert Schweitzer had the following to say about it: "The Devil does not have to keep all the best tunes for himself, Luther once said, and therefore his Christmas carol *Vom Himmel hoch da komm ich her* [*From Heaven above to Earth I come*] is written to the melody of the riddle *Ich komm aus fremden Landen her*, in which the singer presents a puzzle, receiving a wreath from the maiden who cannot solve it. He [Luther] later had to return this melody to the Devil, for even after its conversion it still resounded in all the dancing halls and taverns. Anno 1551 Walter removed it from the hymnbook and replaced it with the tune to which Luther's carol is still sung to this very day."

Page 22/23:
The castle and abbey church form the crown of Quedlinburg – both literally and figuratively. In 929, seven years before his death, King Heinrich I bequeathed Quitilingaburg to his wife Mathilde as her widow's seat. She founded a famous convent here in 937.

Page 24/25:
The church and adjacent town hall in Stendal in the Altmark. St Marien was begun in 1335 and completed in 1447. The town hall is also largely a product of the 15th century.

KaffeeKult

From Zeitz to the Harz

Naumburg Cathedral attracts arts fans from all over the world to the former bishopric on the River Saale. The first church was consecrated in 1042, with the new, late Romanesque place of worship finished exactly 200 years later. Gothic elements were first introduced with the west choir in c. 1250.

The first vineyards were planted under Saxon kings, yet it was the Cistercians of Pforta who really launched the wine-making tradition here. Pfortenser Köppelberg, the oldest vineyard on the Saale and Unstrut rivers still farmed, dates back to the mid 12th century. On its loess, shingle and Muschelkalk soils Gutedel, Müller-Thurgau, Pinot gris, Blauer Silvaner and Blauer Portugieser thrive. The terrain here is very much like Franconia in Bavaria, giving rise to comparable wines that are exceedingly popular. However, this wasn't always the case. In a chronicle from the early 18th century we can read that you needed a certain amount of courage to drink the local vintages. Although they held promise of good health and a long life, the students of Jena never tired of poking fun at their regional tipple. Matthias Claudius in local newspaper *Wandsbecker Bothe* was just one who complained about "... a produce that looks like wine / But 'tis not; you cannot sing while drinking it / Nor become merry on it."

Since 1993 the Straße der Romanik or Romanesque Route has joined 65 historic towns and villages endowed with a rich heritage from the mid 10th to mid 13th centuries. The many sights well worth seeing between the River Saale and Harz Mountains include a number of representative fortified edifices, such as the Moritzburg in Zeitz, the Neuenburg up above Freyburg and the castles in Allstedt, Querfurt and Falkenstein. There are also many famous places of worship, among them Naumburg Cathedral, the abbey churches of St Servatius in Quedlinburg and St Cyriacus in Gernrode and the monastic churches at Memleben, Ilsenburg and Konradsburg.

The scenic high point – in all senses of the word – is the Harz. About 10% of the overall area (24 hectares/60 acres) enjoys special protection. Almost completely swathed in forest, the Harz Mountains National Park was created when its two halves in Lower Saxony (West Germany) and Saxony-Anhalt (East Germany) became one in 2006.

The town hall in Naumburg, a three-storey, late Gothic building, is around 500 years old. The six lucarnes on its front are adorned with blind tracery and semicircular tops.

The spacious market square in Naumburg is surrounded by beautiful houses. In the 14th and 15th centuries Naumburg wasn't just a bishopric but also a major centre of trade where fairs and exhibitions of various goods were held.

Right page:
Wenzelsbrunnen in the southeast corner of the market square is dedicated to the patron saint of Naumburg, St Wenceslas. The statue of the Bohemian saint was added to the well in 1579. It was created by one of the city's illustrious citizens, sculptor Heinrich Hase.

Hotel
Aachen
PAULANER

Right:
Naumburg, Herrenstraße 2. The building with the wonderful façade houses the Lorbeerbaum or laurel tree chemist's, founded in 1645.

Far right:
The main portal of Naumburg's town hall goes back to the beginning of the 17th century.

Right and far right:
Haus von Veit Laube on Markt 10 once welcomed an imperial guest; in 1547 Emperor Karl V lodged here. His two prisoners, Landgrave of Hesse Philipp I (The Magnanimous) and Elector of Saxony Johann Friedrich I, had to make do with the Zum Scheffel inn and St George's Monastery as their temporary abode.

Much of St Wenceslas, a three-storey, late Gothic hall church, was built in an incredibly short period, namely from 1517–1523. The interior has been baroqueified. The main altar (1677–1680) is attributed to Heinrich Schau and the elaborately restored organ from 1746 to Zacharias Hildebrandt.

Beautiful Uta and Saint Elizabeth

Naumburg's prime landmark is without a doubt its cathedral. The foundations of the Romanesque/Gothic house of God were laid in the early 13th century. Muschelkalk from the River Saale was used as the chief building material. The edifice was constructed in sections, with the nave, east towers (with the exception of the baroque domes) and crypt from the late Romanesque period. The west choir is early Gothic, the choir at the east end high Gothic. The west towers, begun in the Romanesque style, were only finished in the 19th century.

This is where time and people are measured in stone. The figures that adorn the west choir in particular are masterpieces – and also a historical and artistic riddle. In c. 1250 Bishop Dietrich II decided to erect a memorial not to saints of the church but to the lay people who donated money to build the church. The commission can't have been easy. The 13th-century artist entrusted with the job was instructed to create statues of two past Ekkeharding margraves, their wives and other nobles from the 11th and 12th centuries with little more than their names to go on. To add to the puzzle the artist himself left no clues as to his identity; his name has become lost in the mists of time.

Whoever he was the Naumburg Master, whose handiwork is also thought to grace the cathedrals of Noyon, Reims, Amiens, Metz, Strasbourg and Mainz, excelled himself. He made the past, both his and ours, a work of permanence – a transformation that even in art is hard to achieve. The fine dimensions of these twelve figures, their natural stance and vivacious expressions have a compelling finality about them. The two stone margraves couldn't be more unlike. On one side is Hermann, the soft-hearted, vulnerable ruler: almost estranged in this world, one of the last knights of chivalry and courtly love. The angular, determined Ekkehard II is a completely different character: a doer, a pusher, someone aiming only for the top. And prepared to go to extremes. His wife, beautiful Uta from Ballenstedt, has turned up one of the collars of her mantel as if to protect herself from her harsh husband. While she seems to look inward Reglindis, the Polish princess, is open and uncomplicated. The Laughing Bride probably gave her dreamy spouse the grounding he needed.

The best time to visit these people in stone and the ornaments that surround them is late in the day when the light is flat. This is when the matt paint lets the limestone seem softer than it is. The bold outlines and concept behind the statues are just as visible as the more subtle traits and the details: here a cloak of wool or linen and a dress of silk, there a leather shoe and a metal sword.

Welcome refuge

Neuenburg just a few kilometres from Naumburg is inextricably linked to the life of another famous lady. The castle was the favourite residence of Saint Elizabeth of Hungary, as she was to become, who came here to escape the noisy court at Wartburg Castle as often as she could. Both castles are said to date back to Ludwig the Leaper. The first major conversions were instigated by Landgrave Hermann, Elizabeth's father-in-law. The keep in front of the inner gate has survived from this period (1225).

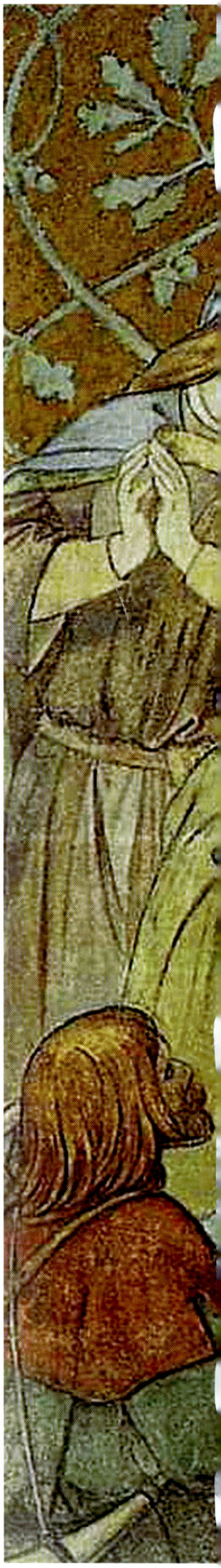

Top far right: *The upper part of the chapel reserved for the landgrave and his family is richly ornamented.*

Right: *The most famous legend surrounding Elizabeth of Hungary is the miracle of the rose, depicted here by Moritz von Schwind.*

Bottom far right: *Minnesinger Heinrich von Veldeke is thought to have died shortly before 1190 at Neuenburg Castle.*

Far left: *Princess Reglindis of Poland was married to Margrave of Meißen Hermann I and therefore Uta's sister-in-law.*

Left: *Uta von Ballenstedt with her husband Ekkehard II, made margrave of Meißen in 1038. They had no children.*

For those interested in medieval art and architecture, the church is a must. Ludwig, Elizabeth's husband, had a second floor added to the existing building. The result is a Romanesque two-storey chapel where everybody could hear the service in one place: the landgrave and his family safely ensconced upstairs, with his subjects crowded in below. The two classes were separated by a mighty ceiling and joined by a tiny sound hole. Now restored, the richly decorated upper floor especially – the ribbed vaulting, transverse chevron arches, clustered central columns and capitals – presents itself in its full beauty and remarkable perfection.

The Rudelsburg is the River Saale's epitome of the romantic – or Romantic – castle. In 1826 it was here that 18-year-old Franz Kugler, the later historian, wrote his famous ode to the river and to the proud and mighty castles that tower above it.

The village of Schulpforte was once a monastery. The Monasterium apud portam was founded in the 12th century by the Cistercians who transformed their swampy surroundings into beautiful gardens. During the period of secularisation the monastery became the royal school of Schulpforta, for centuries one of the most famous seats of learning in Germany. This tradition is now continued by the Pforta state school for gifted children and teenagers. The state winery is also based in Schulpforte.

Left page:
The palace church in Zeitz (originally the cathedral of St Peter and Paul), an aisled hall church that is Romanesque in essence, was converted to late Gothic after 1430 and later baroqueified from the mid 17th century onwards.

Vast, early baroque Schloss Moritzburg in Zeitz was planned by Johann Moritz Richter the Elder. It now houses a very good museum.

Left and far left:
Despite witnessing many wars the rich legacy of Schulpforte has managed to survive, manifested in its church, abbot's chapel, and cloisters.

Page 40/41:
God of wine Bacchus has a small but very pretty holding near Freyburg, where the Saale and Unstrut rivers converge. In the background is Neuenburg Castle.

The literal high point of Freyburg on the River Unstrut is Neuenburg Castle atop a limestone ridge clad in vines. The mightiest stronghold of the landgraves of Thuringia is said to date back to Ludwig the Leaper. Dicker Wilhelm, the only one of three squat towers to survive, is from the second half of the 12th century. The castle was turned into a regal residence under Landgrave Hermann I and his son Ludwig IV, Elizabeth of Hungary's husband. The former also had the impressive residential tower built.

Right:
The Marienkirche in Freyburg, an aisled, late Romanesque hall church at its core, dates back to the start of the 13th century. The new, late Gothic nave was probably built at the end of the 1400s.

Right page:
Red Riding Hood lives in this prestigious dwelling in Freyburg. No, not the girl with the wolfish grandmother from the fairy story by the Brothers Grimm but manufacturers of sparkling wine Rotkäppchen, founded in 1856.

Schloss Neu-Augustusburg in Weißenfels was erected in the second half of the 17th century. In the palace chapel, which boasts an unusually rich stucco array, Friedrich Handel once played the organ as a boy. Another composer since his youth, Johann Beer from Austria, came to the palace as a singer, oversaw the library and was made concertmaster to the court in 1685. He also wrote a series of successful, Simplician, anti-courtly novels under various pseudonyms which only came to light two hundred years after his death.

The old mining town of Sangerhausen has the largest collection of roses in the world. The Europa Rosarium contains about 8,300 different species of the queen of flowers. The gardens covering 12.5 hectares or ca. 30 acres are packed with roses from different countries and periods, many of them absolute rarities.

Below:
Luther's birthplace in Eisleben has been a memorial since the end of the 17th century, making it one of the first museums in Germany. In 1996 the 15th-century edifice was made a UNESCO World Heritage Site.

Right:
View of the marketplace in Eisleben with the statue of Luther on the right. The late Gothic, aisled church of St Andreas dates back to the second quarter of the 15th century. The town hall with its pointed gable, also late Gothic, was completed in 1531.

17 12
Hotel
Weißes Roß
HOTEL
RESTAURANT
Weißes Roß
Hotel Stolberger

Page 52/53:
Small (with just 1,500 inhabitants) but beautiful: Stolberg. The birthplace of theologian and revolutionary Thomas Müntzer is heralded as the pearl of the South Harz. The Saigerturm, the lower stone section of which is from the 1200s, watches over its idyllic, half-timbered centre.

The palace in Stolberg was originally a 10th/11th-century castle, extensively refurbished during the Renaissance and baroque periods. Under the GDR regime the official residence of the counts of Stolberg was a rest home for teachers. After the building was abandoned in 1994 and began to fall into decay, in 2002 it was taken on by the Deutsche Stiftung Denkmalschutz or the German foundation for the preservation of historical monuments. The results are incredible; in 2008 the restored royal wing was opened to the public and in 2009 the palace chapel opened its doors.

Stolberg has about 400 half-timbered buildings from five centuries, 18 of which are pre-1530. Each and every one is different.

The timberwork in Stolberg is so beautiful that even the likes of Goethe and Heine were spellbound by it.

Left:
The abbey church of St Cyriakus in Gernrode is one of the most magnificent examples of Ottonian architecture in Germany. The convent was founded in 961 by Margrave Gero on the site of his castle of Geronisroth. The foundations for the church were probably laid two years prior to this.

Below:
Schloss Ballenstedt goes back to the counts of Anhalt-Bernburg who had the baroque palace erected in the first half of the 18th century on the foundations of a Benedictine monastery. A section of abbey's westwork was integrated into the palace walls.

Above:
The town hall in Quedlinburg was first mentioned in 1310. 300 years later it was given a new Renaissance façade. The statue of Roland from 1427 was pulled down half a century later and only reinstated in 1869.

Right:
Finkenherd or the 'forest' of finches in Quedlinburg. This is where Heinrich, duke of Saxony, is said to have heard that he had been elected ruler of the East Frankish Kingdom in 919.

Above:
There are plenty of cafés and restaurants dotted around the marketplace in Quedlinburg. On the left is part of the town hall.

Left:
Lange Gasse close to Finkenherd also boasts many historical half-timbered dwellings.

Above:
The roofs of Quedlinburg seen from Schlossberg. The city evolved from a trading post which Emperor Otto III awarded the right to hold markets, mint coins and levy taxes to at the end of the 10th century.

Right:
Half-timbering on Schlossberg or the castle mound. A royal edifice first stood atop the elongated sandstone ridge as long ago as in 800. A few decades later a chapel was built which was to become the forerunner of the abbey church.

Left:
The abbey church of St Servatius in Quedlinburg, consecrated in 1129, is one of the absolute highlights of Romanesque art and architecture in Germany. Both King Heinrich I and his wife Mathilde, who founded the convent, were laid to rest here.

Below:
The half-timbered baroque houses on Marktkirchhof were put up at the end of the 17th century. This is where local policemen, midwives and the city waits (band of musicians) lived.

The Cistercian monastery of Michaelstein a few kilometres west of Blankenburg goes back to the mid 12th century. Following its destruction in the Peasant Wars the church had to be torn down. The enclosure with its early Gothic cloister (c. 1270) has survived and now houses an interesting museum of musical instruments, among other things.

Above:
The Kleines Schloss or small palace in Blankenburg has a pretty baroque garden. It was laid out in 1725, complete with fountains, statues, a grotto and a copy of the famous Brunswick Lion.

Far left:
The present town hall in Blankenburg was erected at the beginning of the 16th century to replace the previous building from the 14th/15th centuries. The second floor was only added in 1584.

Left:
The town of Blankenburg evolved beneath the castle of the same name. The village was granted its town charter (Goslar Rights) in the 14th century.

Legend has it that the Harz almost belonged to the Devil. In the battle over property God promised that if the Prince of Darkness had erected a boundary wall around the mountains by the first cockcrow at dawn, the hills were his. However, an extremely punctual rooster in Cattenstedt gave the signal too early. The Devil was so angry he smashed his work to pieces, leaving half of it standing. The remains are now known as the Teufelsmauer or Devil's Wall.

The cathedral of St Stephanus and St Sixtus in Halberstadt is one of Germany's Gothic highlights. It was begun in the middle of the 13th century and finally consecrated in 1491. The west towers were added in 1896. It took until 1960 for the heavy damage inflicted during the Second World War to be repaired.

Left:
The Liebfrauenkirche in Halberstadt was commissioned by Augustinian canons. The first building is thought to go back to the start of the 11th century. During the 1100s the Romanesque place of worship was refurbished and modelled on the abbey in Hirsau.

Below:
After being destroyed during World War II, in 2004 the town hall in Halberstadt was finally restored to its former glory.

Right page:
Westerburg, about 15 kilometres or 9 miles northeast of Osterwieck, dates back to the Carolingian period and is the oldest moated castle still standing in Germany. The keep was constructed in the 11th century.

In the little town of Osterwieck there is a half-timbered house for every ten inhabitants (the population is around 4,000). The steeples in the background belong to the Romanesque section of the now Gothic parish church of St Stephani.

This fine example of half-timbering is from 1579: Wolfs Brauhaus zum Güldenen Löwen, the Golden Lion brewery pub on Schützenstraße.

Page 74/75:
The palace in Wernigerode is like something out of a fairytale. The ancestral seat of the counts of Stolberg and Wernigerode took on its present guise in the 19th century. The plans for its conversion were drawn up by Karl Frühling from Brunswick.

Below:
View of the marketplace, the showcase of Wernigerode. The town grew up around the castle and profited from its location at the intersection of two trade routes and military roads. In 1229 it was granted its Goslar town charter.

Top right:
The town hall in Wernigerode is richly decorated with ornaments and figures. No less than 33 minstrels, storytellers, dancers, fools and saints look down on passers by from the beams above.

Centre right: *Wernigerode's town hall, which was given its present design at the end of the 15th century by Thomas Hilleborch, has twice featured on German stamps (in 1961 and 2000).*

Bottom right: *Ancient half-timbered houses on Kochstraße. This cheerful town in the Harz owes its colour to the multitude of wooden-framed edifices here. The smallest, also on Kochstraße, is just 2.95 m (9.68 ft) wide and 4.20 m (13.78 ft) high.*

Ghosts, Witches and Poets – Brocken Mountain

The Brocken Ghost is one of those beings from the other world that is quite promiscuous. Unlike many other ghouls, there's absolutely no doubt that it exists. It only appears at sunrise and sunset – and only in certain weather conditions and if at least one person is present. When the sun projects its shadow onto a bank of fog, it moves, changes and comes alive, surrounded by a strange and eerie light. In damp fog it is "enveloped by a colourful shimmer" and in frost it reflects "a yellow, brilliant light", according to Marie Kutschman in her book *Im Zauberbann des Harzgebirges* (Under the Spell of the Harz Mountains) from 1890.

Even if meteorologists and physicists have long fathomed the phantom, Brocken Mountain is still extremely dangerous. Or at least Magister Johannes Praetorius from the Altmark claimed in his book from 1668 *Blockes-Berges Verrichtung* (Blockberg Phenomena), in which he describes the physical presence of evil on earth. Praetorius wrote, "The Blocksberg or Brocken ... is very famous throughout Germany for its witches and fiends, who each year on Walpurgis Night or the first of May hold convention or court there, coming together from places far afield ..." And he continues, in rhyme, to describe what they get up to, these witches with their devilish brood, dancing, leaping, drinking and cavorting with evil spirits.

Goethe was familiar with this book and referred on several occasions to Praetorius as the man who "loves strange figures". In order to gain an impression for himself he climbed the mountain no less than three times: in 1777, 1783 and 1784. His friend and patron Johann Heinrich Merck learned that on December 8, 1777, at one o'clock in the afternoon, he stood "on top of the Brocken in the brightest, most burning sun, on snow one-and-a-half cubits high, and saw the area of Germany beneath me, all covered in cloud". Three decades later, on Walpurgis Night, he sent Faust and Mephistopheles up the mountain, marking the Brocken's entry into the annals of literary history.

Another famous poet, Heinrich Heine, has a monument erected in his honour on the mountain. As a student he travelled from Göttingen to the Harz Mountains near Ilsenburg. During his four-week tour he also ventured up the mountain where he had the landlord wake him specially so that he could watch the sunrise. As he recalls in his poem *Auf dem Brocken* (On Brocken Mountain), his thoughts were elsewhere – namely with his lady love.

Mountain of extremes

Even if writer and schoolmaster Heinrich Pröhle claims to have met many "ugly, witch-like women" in the village of Schierke at the foot of Brocken Mountain in the mid 19th century, the Brocken's association with witches' covens is surely not founded on these poor females but on the extreme weather conditions that prevail here. The Harz may only be in the medium mountain range but this counts for little once you've mastered the 1,141 metres (3,744 feet) of the Brocken. At the top everything changes. The climatic conditions are the same as on mountains 1,800 to 2,200 metres (6,000 to 7,000 feet) high; the flora is comparable to that

Right: *The Walpurgis Night scene from Goethe's Faust. Copper engraving by Wilhelm Jury after Johann Heinrich Ramberg.*

Top far right: *The hikers have finally made it to the summit (1951).*

Centre far right: *This 'experiment' was performed in 1932 to see how much truth there was in the saga that a billy goat could be turned into a beautiful young man by a virgin of pure heart – in the light of a full moon, of course.*

Bottom far right: *Walpurgis Night, 1932. As you can see, all that's real about these witches and wizards are their broomsticks.*

Far left: *The summit of Brocken Mountain in c. 1900. The hotel was built in 1862 after the old Brockenhaus burned down.*

Left: *Two steam engines are needed to pull the carriages of the Brockenbahn up the mountain (between 1890 and 1905).*

of Northern Scandinavia and the Alps. The winters are very long, the summers all the shorter. The lowest temperature measured here was -28.4°C, the highest wind speed 263 kilometres (163 miles) an hour and the deepest snow 3.8 metres (12.4 feet). In 1958 Brocken Mountain was shrouded in fog for an unbelievable 330 days. On average this is every third day in the year. Whereas Goethe and Heine had to climb the mountain on foot, people visiting the Brocken after 1899 were able to travel by mountain railway. This was until 1961 when the area became a prohibited military zone. The trains only started operating a regular service again in 1992.

99 7234-0

Left page:
The first train reached the top of Brocken Mountain on March 27, 1899 – without a cogged track or any other aid. The narrow-gauge steam engines have a strength of around 700 horse power.

The Brocken is often hidden from view, its presence felt rather than actually visible in the frequent fog and low cloud here. It's a rare occasion when the summit is clear and the views are as splendid as this.

In the 1990s this stone was instated on the top of the Brocken marking its height (1,142 m/3,747 ft). Behind it are the radio tower and Brockenhaus which were once used to listen in on calls made by the citizens of the GDR.

The winters on Brocken Mountain are long, harsh, snowy and stormy. The average temperature starts to sink below zero in November. The coldest month is usually February with an average of -4.7°C.

In March the air is still a chilly -2°C. The sun doesn't often make it through the clouds, yet when it does the views of glittering fields of snow and magical, windswept trees are almost unreal.

Near Thale, high up above the deep gorge of Bodetal, is the legendary spot where the witches of the Brocken are said to converge. They have to resort to broomsticks as their mode of transport; modern-day visitors can take the more comfortable cable car.

The towers of Halle. Next to the statue of Handel is the Roter Turm or red tower, erected in 1418 in the centre of the market square as a symbol of civic pride. In the background is the Church of Our Lady.

The twin towers once belonged to two different churches; after these were pulled down they were joined by an aisled nave to form the present market church in 1554.

The brown coal mines and chemical giants around Merseburg, Halle and Bitterfeld not only blacken the villages and surrounding countryside but also the name of an entire region, harming both its people and environment. On the closure of the pits the fresh air returned but the jobs went. In the meantime a lot has happened. New, modern industries have become established and the Earth's scars have started to heal. Extensive naturalisation projects have turned old mining areas into green woods and glittering lakes. Nowhere else in the former German Democratic Republic has the scenery changed so dramatically.

If Magister Michael Stifel had been right, Saxony-Anhalt – and indeed the Earth itself – would no longer exist. The monk predicted that the world would end at 8 am on October 19, 1533. It didn't. Instead, those who had waited tremulously in the electoral seat of Lochau (later Annaburg) near Wittenberg for the skies to darken forever wanted to end something else: Stifel's life. He was arrested for his own protection yet wasn't charged for the damage he had caused with his false prognosis. His friend Luther made sure that the electoral coffers – in other words, the tax payer – coughed up in lieu.

In Stifel's defence it must be said that he didn't make any more predictions – even when he embarked on a second career as a mathematician and anticipated today's logarithm tables in his book *Arithmetica integra*. The student song *Stiefel muss sterb*en (Sti(e)fel must die) has since cemented his fame – or infamy.

The counts of Zerbst were "very, very merry men", according to writer Karl Emil Franzos (in *Aus Anhalt und Thüringen*, 1903). In 1797 the fun came to an end, however, when Anhalt-Zerbst completely disappeared off the map. In other words, it was divided up between other rulers – and its capital incredibly sold off at a raffle ...

telecolumbus
telecolumbus
LÜHR
Modellbau
RENO

__Left page:__
Halle, first mentioned in 806, is now the largest city in Saxony-Anhalt and an important centre of industry, education and research with a population of 230,000. Here, Große Ulrichstraße.

Halle's Martin Luther University was founded in 1817 when two other seats of learning merged: the Leucorea in Wittenberg (established in 1502) and the Friedrich University in Halle (opened in 1694).

View of the courtyard of the Moritzburg in Halle. The foundations of the fortifications and palace named after the state's patron saint, St Mauritius, were laid in 1484 by Archbishop Ernst II of Wettin. In the background on the right is the chapel dedicated to Mary Magdalene.

The plans for the late Gothic, aisled Church of Our Lady on the marketplace were drawn up by Caspar Kraft and Nickel Hofmann. The ornate interior is adorned with elaborate fan and stellar vaulting.

The first wooden statue of Roland in Halle burned down. The second was erected in stone in 1719. The third likeness, a copy, was installed on the east flank of the Roter Turm 2006.

Right page:
Market stall in Halle, framed by the Roter Turm and Church of Our Lady on the marketplace. The east towers, linked by a bridge, are known as the Hausmannstürme or houseman's towers, and the west are called the Blue Towers.

NICOLAS FRUIT
Lamanna

Right page:
View across the River Saale of the cathedral and castle in Merseburg. This is where the tale of Moritz Wilhelm of Saxony-Merseburg is set, aka the Fiddling Duke. He was a passionate music lover, collecting every kind of string instrument he could find. He not only played first fiddle in his country but also in his own orchestra and even in church. Bits of the sermon he found particularly pleasing were met with a tune on his violin – and a bottle of wine for the priest.

The castle in Merseburg was built between 1470 and 1537. Its appearance changed with the tastes, needs and financial means of its owners. Bishop Thilo von Trotha, for example, had the north and east wings rebuilt in late Gothic while Duke Moritz had it converted into a more modern style by his master builder Melchior Brenner in the 17th century. Brenner also transformed the castle bailey into one of the most beautiful courtyards of the German Renaissance.

Right and below left:
The late Gothic church of St Jakob in Köthen is where the regents of the local royal house found their final resting place in the 17th and 18th centuries. Johann Sebastian Bach, probably with his wife and son Wilhelm Friedemann, once played and directed the funereal "Klagt, Kinder, klage es aller Welt" here in memory of his patron Leopold.

Far right:
In the course of its long history Köthen has had four town halls, all built on the same site. The first dates back to the 13th century, with the present edifice from 1894–1900.

Right page:
Goitzschesee near Bitterfeld has not been here that long; flooding of the old brown coal mining area only began in 1998. The new lake district is about 13 km² (5 sq miles) in size and up to 48 m (158 ft) deep.

Schloss Reinharz in Bad Schmiedeberg was constructed between 1690 and 1701. The baroque moated castle was commissioned by hereditary marshal of Saxony Heinrich Löser. In the middle of the 18th century the ground floor was restyled in Dresden Rococo.

Baroque Schloss Mosigkau (1754–1756) was probably designed by Georg Wenzeslaus von Knobelsdorff. The picture gallery includes works by Rubens, van Dyck and Jordaens. The preserved Rococo gardens were laid out by Johann Georg Schoch and Christoph Friedrich Brose.

Above:
Schloss Georgium in Dessau goes back to Friedrich Wilhelm von Erdmannsdorff. The two-storey, neoclassical palace, erected after 1780, also has a grand collection of paintings and around 30,000 graphics executed by Cranach, Baldung Grien, Brueghel, Rubens, Hals and others.

Right:
Prince of Anhalt-Dessau Leopold I, better known as The Old Dessauer, in bronze on Schlossplatz in Dessau. The marble original was sculpted by Johann Gottfried Schadow. In the background is the Marienkirche.

Left:
Only the west wing or Johann Building of Dessau's old residential palace, once inhabited by the princes and dukes of Anhalt, has survived the Second World War. The wonderful, early Renaissance structure has been home to the museum of city history since 1999.

Below:
The neoclassical Luisium country house in Dessau-Jonitz was built by Friedrich Wilhelm von Erdmannsdorff between 1774 and 1778. On its completion Johann Friedrich Eyserbeck, Leopold Friedrich Franz III's royal gardener, laid out the park.

The architectural high point and centrepiece of the Bauhaus in Dessau, which consists of several buildings, is the workshop wing with its full glass façade. The vocational school (with its bands of triple windows), studio building (with its balconies) and festive area complete the ensemble.

BAUHAUS

BAUHAUS

The Modern Age in Dessau: the Bauhaus

There aren't many places that can boast not one but two top UNESCO World Heritage Sites. Dessau-Roßlau (the two towns were joined in 2007) is one of them. The first site is the Garden Kingdom of Dessau-Wörlitz that Prince Leopold Friedrich Franz III and his friend Friedrich Wilhelm von Erdmannsdorff laid out in the second half of the 18th century. The second monument is Walter Gropius et al's Bauhaus from the 1920s which has left its distinctive mark on the world, pumping incredible impetus into Modernist architecture and design.

The Bauhaus was founded by Gropius in Weimar in 1919. His answer to the demands of the age was to bring about a reunion of the arts and crafts. Building was for him "the ultimate goal of all fine art ... Modern man, in his modern, not historical guise, also requires a modern home that befits him and his epoch, complete with all the objects of daily use common to our present time." The "Bauhaus wishes to aid the contemporary development of housing, from the simple household appliance to the finished home."

To this end Gropius found various masters to work with him whose names read like a *Who's Who* of the Modern Age: Kandinsky and Schlemmer, Klee and Feininger, Mies van der Rohe, Meyer, Itten, Moholy-Nagy and Muche. The latter built the Haus am Horn in Weimar which was to act as a model for an entire housing estate. Yet it didn't get beyond the drawing board; the government of Thuringia eventually cut all funding for the Bauhaus.

Building and design

Dessau offered itself as an alternative, where Social Democrats and Liberals decided city affairs. Aircraft company Junkers also held promise of money and support. Many ideas and projects, which made history as prototypes for modern building and design, were thus realised at the Hochschule for Gestaltung or school of design. But there was also criticism and attack, causing Gropius to stand down as director in 1928. His successor was Swiss architect Hanns Meyer who was suspected of harbouring Marxist sympathies, however, and rudely thrown out two years later. Ludwig Mies van der Rohe then took over, turning the Bauhaus into a kind of technical university where the architects set the tone, with teams of artists and craftsmen working under them. Mies van der Rohe didn't have much time. In January 1932 the city fathers of Dessau had to decide whether to tear down the college building and sack its staff or not. "The Bauhaus can in no way be brought into line with the term 'German art'. It practises a completely Oriental style of building. It has the tendency to demean ancient, genuine German art, instead producing a sorry effort that hits the German soul and German feeling right in the face", is how the press quoted National Socialist MP Hofmann. When the Nazis came to power, the "sorry effort" remained standing but the teachers and

Top left:
The Stahlhaus or Steel House erected in 1926/27 is a joint effort by Richard Paulick and Georg Muche.

Centre left:
Kornhaus, a country pub on the River Elbe, was designed by Carl Fieger.

their students had to go. Mies van der Rohe, who tried to carry on in Berlin, soon realised he had lost the fight and gave up.

As one of the earliest examples of Modernist architecture the Bauhaus in Dessau attracts visitors from all over the world. The same goes for the Masters' Houses where Gropius, Moholy-Nagy, Feininger, Klee, Kandinsky, Muche and Schlemmer lived and worked. Other places of pilgrimage for Bauhaus fans are the housing estate in Dessau-Törten and a number of other buildings, such as the former employment office and Kornhaus restaurant.

Bottom left:
The Bauhaus canteen next to Kornhaus restaurant still serves its original function.

Above:
Georg and Elsa Muche and Oskar and Tut Schlemmer lived in this Masters' House in Dessau-Törten.

Top right:
Walter Gropius once proclaimed, "Architects, painters, sculptors, we must all return to crafts!"

Right:
Paul Klee came from Weimar to Dessau in 1926 and left again in 1931.

Left page:

The Venus Temple in the Garden Kingdom of Dessau-Wörlitz replaced the previous wooden building at the end of the 18th century. The temple's goddess of love is modelled on Medici's famous sculpture.

View of Palladio Bridge, also known as the White Bridge or Step Bridge, on the Kleines Walloch. Andreas Palladio was an Italian architect whose designs were emulated by von Erdmannsdorff, the builder of this bridge in Wörlitz.

Exploring the Garden Kingdom, also known as the English Grounds of Wörlitz, by gondola sheds a new perspective on its magnificent buildings, sculptures and gardens.

"It is infinitely beautiful here; yesterday evening I was very moved as we stole past the lakes, canals and forests as to how the gods have enabled the prince to surround himself with such a dream", enthused Goethe of his visit to the Garden Kingdom of Dessau-Wörlitz in 1778. Above is the front of the Gothic house, with the Venus Temple below.

Page 108/109: *The market square in Wittenberg, lit up at night. On the left is the Renaissance town hall, built between 1570 and 1573, with the westwork of the city church of St Marien behind it, itself a product of the 14th century.*

The palaces and parks in the Garden Kingdom of Dessau-Wörlitz have been a UNESCO World Heritage Site since November 2000. This magnificent array that hugs the banks of the River Elbe covers almost 150 km² (58 sq miles). Above is the back of the Gothic House, with the Flora Temple below right.

Chagall
Pechstein
Picasso
Dix
Beckmann
u.a.
JOS HENDRICKX
Ausstellung
9.7.- 25.9.2011

Cafe am Markt
ATLAS

Seid fleißig zu halten
die Einigkeit im Geiste
durch das Band
des Friedens.
Ephes. 4. 3.
WELT

Left page:
They may not have always shared the same opinion while they were alive but in bronze they stand united on Wittenberg's marketplace: Martin Luther and Philipp Melanchthon, the two intellectual leaders of the Reformation.

Visible for miles, the mighty steeple of the palace church dominates the west of Old Wittenberg. The castle was first mentioned at the end of the 12th century; the town was granted its charter in 1293.

Left:
The irregularly shaped, late Renaissance palace in Coswig, erected on the foundations of an older castle, was finished in 1677 and served as a widow's seat until the 19th century.

Below:
Near Coswig. The town has a population of around 13,000, a ferry across the River Elbe, a mooring for passenger boats and even a marina, opened in 2007.

Page 114/115:
The Elbe with Coswig in the background. Cossewiz Castle was first mentioned at the end of the 12th century and the town in 1215. It was the most important holding of the Anhalt Ascanians north of the Elbe.

From Magdeburg to the north

Magdeburg's Alter Markt with its famous rider dating back to the mid 13th century, the first freestanding statue of a man on horseback north of the Alps. Behind him is the baroque town hall (1691–1698) which was painstakingly rebuilt to its original design after the Second World War.

Unlike the Landshut Wedding the Magdeburger Hochzeit or Magdeburg 'Wedding' wasn't a superlative royal feast but a cynical term for a heinous crime. After seizing the city on May 20, 1631, the troops of the Catholic League 'married' the rebellious town to the emperor. This meant that his henchmen sacked the city so thoroughly that hardly anybody survived and Magdeburg was almost completely erased from the map. The worst massacre in the course of the Thirty Years' War, that prompted history books and dictionaries to coin the phrase "magdeburgisation", cost at least 20,000 people their lives. Some sources put this figure at 30,000.

Magdeburg was badly hit again during the Second World War. Following the raid by the British Royal Air Force on January 16, 1944, almost the entire city lay in ruins. 2,000 died in the inferno; ten times that number lost their homes. During the GDR era only a few architectural monuments were rebuilt, among them the cathedral, the monastery of Our Lady and the town hall. After the fall of the Berlin Wall the city's main axis Breiter Weg, Domplatz, Friedensplatz and other major streets were revamped to the joy of its 230,000 inhabitants and their many guests.

As chance would have it, the central area of countryside in Saxony-Anhalt has the same name as its state capital. The Magdeburg Börde, an extremely fertile legacy of the ice age with some of it covered in black earth or chernozem soil, is perfect for wheat and sugar beet. In the north it runs into the Altmark and to the east into the Fläming, a high ridge 100 kilometres (60 miles) long and 50 kilometres (30 miles) wide, part of which belongs to the German federal state of Brandenburg. Old chronicles long referred to the area as the Sächsischer Grenzwall or Saxon Boundary; today's name goes back to the 15th century and the Flemish colonists who moved here after the founding of the march.

No less than five streets converge on Hasselbachplatz in Magdeburg, named after a local mayor of long standing. The Gründerzeit buildings that surround it have long been given a new splash of colour, housing all kinds of shops, pubs and bars.

Above:
The Grüne Zitadelle or green citadel in Magdeburg is one of the greatest and last works by Friedensreich Hundertwasser. The artist saw his creation as "an oasis for humanity and nature in a sea of rational housing".

Far left:
The old post office is now a law centre named after Eike von Repgow. The Anhalt noble wrote the first book of law in the German language between 1220 and 1230, entitled the "Sachsenspiegel".

Left:
This statue of Otto von Guericke dates from 1907. At his feet lie the famous Magdeburg hemispheres.

Left page and far left:
The cathedral of St Mauritius and St Katharina in Magdeburg is a real gem of sacred medieval architecture. Hardly anything remains of its Ottonian predecessor which burned down in 1207. The new Gothic house of God was begun just two years later and consecrated in 1363. The interior of the cathedral is just as impressive. Work on the rood screen began in 1445; the westwork was completed around 70 years later.

The parish church of St Johannis on Alter Markt in Magdeburg was turned into a late Gothic, aisled hall church in the 15th century. The only Romanesque section to have survived is the westwork from the 1100s.

South of the cathedral is the enclosure with its cloister where interesting tombstones from the 14th to 19th centuries have been preserved.

Above:
In 1945 baroque Schloss Hundisburg was used as a barracks by the Red Army and much of it burned down. The town of Haldensleben has since restored it to its former beauty, complete with its baroque gardens.

Right:
Of the three gates in the Hanseatic town of Gardelegen only the Salzwedeler Tor from c. 1550 still stands. The two mighty gun towers were added in the 17th century.

Far right:
A stone Roland also protects the wellbeing of the town of Haldensleben. The town hall dates back to 1703. It was given its neo-classical design in 1823.

Above:
Letzlingen hunting lodge (Hirschburg) was put up in the mid 16th century by Elector Johann Georg von Brandenburg. Around 400 years later Friedrich Wilhelm IV of Prussia had it rebuilt in the neo-Gothic style.

Left and far left:
In Bad Salzelmen, now part of Schönebeck, salt was mined for over eight centuries. The first salt spa in Germany opened here in 1802. The thorn house, 1,837 m (6,027 ft) long, was the largest ever built. About 350 m (1,148 ft) of it are still left. In 1878 the Lindenbad spa rooms replaced an older bathing facility.

A TRANQUIL AND BEAUTIFUL PLACE – THE ALTMARK

The Altmark, at 4,500 square kilometres (1,737 square miles) almost twice the size of the German federal state of the Saarland, stretches from the Magdeburg Börde in the south to the Wendland. It is bordered to the east by the River Elbe and in the west by the hilly Drawehn. While the south is largely made up of forest and pastureland, the north is a patchwork of fields. The area used to be covered in inaccessible swamp which was gradually drained with great effort. Anything but inviting in the Middle Ages, the land to the west of the Elbe only gained (strategic) importance during the expansion of Germany to the east, forming the nucleus of the March of Brandenburg established in the middle of the 12th century. Describing it as the "cradle of the Prussian state", as some Wilhelmine lexica do, is thus more a question of patriotism than geography. Curiously, it was a Prussian king, namely Friedrich Wilhelm I, who warned of his "vassals in the Altmark"; as opposed to his Pomeranians, who were "as true as gold", the Altmark was full of "bad, disobedient people". His successor to the throne was urgently advised to watch out for them. Of the noble families, the Soldier King said, the "Schulenburgs, Alvenslebens and Bismarcks" were the most dangerous. His maxim was that if you treated them well, then Heaven help you ...

As Fate would have it, it was indeed a Bismarck – Otto Eduard Leopold von Bismarck to be precise, born on April 1, 1815, in Schönhausen in the Altmark – who was to shame the king posthumously when as imperial chancellor he was largely instrumental in establishing Prussia not only as the ruler of the German Empire but also as a central European power. This makes it easier to understand the brave people of Poppau who believe the distinctive monolith erected in their region to be the hub of the universe. Georg Bötticher, the father of the Joachim who rose to literary fame under the name of Ringelnatz, made up a rhyme about it: "Any nest, however small, sees / itself as the centre of the world ..."

Balm for the soul

The fact that the completion and activation of the largest atomic power station in Germany near Stendal became redundant when Germany was reunited was an absolute blessing for the Altmark. The expansive, tranquil countryside is now free to laud the many assets its visitors love without any ifs and buts. The region is both rich in natural beauty and balm for the soul; the expression "green tourism" is in no danger of becoming an overused slogan here. The cobbled roads which have survived the past require care and attention, forcing both motorists and cyclists to drive slowly. The villages are charming but not overtly prettified. Many of the churches are built from stones found in the fields. Half-timbering is also in abundance. The flat, slightly hilly landscape is reminiscent of North Germany, as are the towns, of which Stendal is the largest with a population of 42,000. Its people once rose to prosperity through foreign trade, the legacy of which is evident in the town's fine, red-brick, Gothic churches, town hall and gateways. Stendal was a member of the Hanseatic League, as were Werben, Seehausen, Osterburg, Havelberg, Salzwedel, Gardelegen and Tangermünde. The latter is famous for having the largest church in the Altmark, St Stephen's, an impressive castle from the period of Emperor Karl IV, who made the town one of his royal seats, and wonderful half-timbered houses. Not far away, just 13 kilometres (8 miles) to be exact, a Romanesque gem awaits. The church of Jerichow Abbey is one of the most magnificent bequests of this period in Germany.

Left:
As the name suggests, Tangermünde ("Tanger estuary") is where the River Tanger flows into the River Elbe. In the background is the castle keep.

Above:
The Elbe near Grieben, a village to the west of the river with just 800 inhabitants.

Small photos, right, from top to bottom: *The Zur Post restaurant on Langer Straße in Tangermünde.*

The Altmark looks especially pretty when the poppies are in bloom.

The idyllic Altmark: the serene River Elbe surrounded by lush green meadows.

With an area of ca. 514 hectares (1,270 acres) Arendsee is the largest natural lake in Saxony-Anhalt.

Page 126/127:
View of Tangermünde. On the left is the parish church of St Stephan, one of the outstanding creations of the North German Gothic brick period. To the right are the towers of the castle.

Top left page:
The castle in Tangermünde was converted into a minor residential seat for Emperor Karl IV and changed again in the 15th century. It burned down in 1640. One of the sections to have survived is the keep.

Far left:
Neustädter Tor in Tangermünde from c. 1450 is very distinctive with its ornate blind tracery.

Left:
The old gatehouse of the castle in Tangermünde was also used as a dungeon, hence the name Gefängnisturm or prison tower.

Far left:
The old town hall in Tangermünde was built by Hinrich Brunsberg who also erected the Katharinenkirche in Brandenburg.

Left:
A marvellous example of late Romanesque architecture can be found in the church at the old Premonstratensian abbey of Jerichow. Much of the aisled, pillared basilica was erected in the second half of the 12th century.

Bottom left page:
Tangermünde not only has plenty of splendid Gothic brick buildings to offer; many of its streets and excellently restored half-timbered houses from the 17th and 18th centuries are also well worth seeing.

Right:
Brick neighbours: in the foreground is Stendal's town hall, largely a product of the 15th century, with its giant statue of Roland. In the background you can see the towers of the parish church of St Marien (c. 1345–1447).

Below:
Stendal was first mentioned in 1022. In 1160 it was granted its market rights by Albrecht I (The Bear), margrave of Brandenburg. Uenglinger Tor (c. 1450/1460) in the northwest of the old town is one of the most impressive city gates of the Gothic brick period.

Page 132/133:
The River Tanger widening at the harbour just before it flows into the Elbe, seen from the town walls of Tangermünde.

DDR-657
35
Ali Baba

Index

20 km
Prignitz
Perleberg
Dannenberg
Wittenberge
Lüchow
Wendland
Jelzen
Pollitz
Neuruppin
Elbe
Seehausen
Arendsee
Werben
Marienkirche
Salzwedel
Dom
Havelberg
Sandau
Dähre
Mahlsdorf
Osterburg
Oranienburg
Altmärker
Freilichtmuseum
Diesdorf
Jeetze
Wittingen
Schollene
Messdorf
Goldbeck
Rohrberg
Beetzendorf
Arneburg
Havel
Bismark
Klietz
Land Schollene
Borstel
NIEDER-
SACHSEN
Kalbe
Rathenow
Nauen
Klötze
Stendal
Dom
Altmark
Schönhausen
Bismarck-Museum
Grenzmuseum
Böckwitz
Kusey
Tangermünde
Premnitz
Rathaus
Jävenitz
Gardelegen
Rathaus
Lüderitz
BERLIN
Klosterkirche
Jerichow
Colbitz-
Letzlinger
Heide
Mieste
Schlagenthin
Drömling
Havel
Tanger-
hütte
WOLFSBURG
Genthin
Brandenburg
Oebisfelde
Calvörde
Burgstall
Parey
SACHSEN-
Flechtingen
Rogätz
Schloss Detzel
Colbitz
Weferlingen
Tucheim
BRAUNSCHWEIG
Haldensleben
Burg
BRANDENBURG
Helmstedt
Bebertal
Wolmirstedt
Erxleben
Groß-
Ammensleben
Schiffshebewerk
Wefensleben
Kulturhistor.
Museum
Agrarmuseum
Eichen-
barleben
Ummendorf
Möckern
Magdeburger Börde
Dom
MAGDEBURG
Luckenwalde
Hohen-
dodeleben
Seehausen
Gommern
Nedlitz
Hoher Fläming
Schloss
Leitzkau
Hamersleben
Wanzleben
Magdeburger Börde
Schönebeck
Dedeleben
Oschersleben
Serno
Bode
Hadmersleben
Klosterkirche
Zerbst
Dardesheim
Osterwieck
Gröningen
Zarin-Katharina-
Museum
Barby
Zahna
Kloster
Huysburg
Huy
Egeln
Hakel
Holtemme
Roßlau
Coswig
Lutherstadt
Wittenberg
Förderstedt
Elbe
Goslar
Halberstadt
Calbe
Schloss
Georgium
Luisium
Wörlitzer Park
Ilsenburg
Schloss
Derenburg
Wegeleben
Kloster
Hecklingen
Stassfurt
Aken
Dessau
Wörlitz
Bauhaus
Schloss
Rathaus
Wernigerode
Ruine
Regenstein
Ditfurt
Kloster
Nienburg
Mulde
Jessen
Schloss
Brocken
1142 m
Blankenburg
Quedlinburg
Güsten
Bernburg
Kemberg
Elbe
St. Stephani
Schloss
Gräfen-
hainichen
Baggersee
Ferropolis
Annaburg
Thale
Rosenburg
Aschersleben
Köthen
Bad
Schmiede-
berg
Elbingerode
Baumannshöhle
Bergtheater
Falkenstein
Annaburger
Heide
Harz
Bode
Rappbode
Stausee
Hexentanzplatz
Ballenstedt
Alsleben
ANHALT
Zschornewitz
Raguhn
Schloss
Lichtenburg
Treseburg
Burg Falkenstein
Gröbzig
Prettin
Hasselfelde
Burg Anhalt
Burg Arnstein
Saale
Könnern
Wolfen
Dübener
Heide
Hettstedt
Zörbig
Bitterfeld
Harzgerode
Mansfeld
Gerbstedt
Rammelburg
Kloster
Mansfeld
Wettin
Schloss
Wippra
Stolberg
Wipper
Helbra
Landsberg
Burg
Giebichenstein
Delitzsch
Thyragrotte
Rottleberode
Eisleben
Luther-
häuser
Halle
Neustadt
HALLE
Dom
Händelhaus
Nordhausen
Sangerhausen
Röblingen
Teutschenthal
Kelbra
Saale
Goldene Aue
Bad
Lauchstädt
Schkopau
Allstedt
Schloss
Querfurt
Schloss
Dom
Merseburg
Burg
Querfurt
Geiseltalsee
Bad
Dürrenberg
Sondershausen
LEIPZIG
Unstrut
Mulde
Schloss
Nebra
Mücheln
Braunsbedra
Museum
Arche Nebra
Zwenkau
Laucha
Freyburg
SACHSEN
Bad Bibra
Neuenburg
Augustus-
burg
Weissenfels
THÜRINGEN
Dom
Naumburg
Hohenmölsen
Sömmerda
Bad Kösen
Ruine
Rudelsburg
Teuchern
Eckartsberga
Ruine Saaleck
Osterfeld
Moritzburg
Zeitz
Droyßig
Apolda
Ilm
Kayna
Altenburg
ERFURT
Weiße Elster
WEIMAR
Saale
GOTHA
JENA
GERA
CHEMNITZ

The German name "Elend" ("misery") – here the station building in the well-known spa of Elend – probably comes from Old High German "alia landa" which means outside the country, lonely, in the wasteland.

Journey through Saxony-Anhalt

Design
www.hoyerdesign.de

Map
Fischer Kartografie, Aichach

Translation
Ruth Chitty, Stromberg
www.rapid-communication.de

Printed in Germany
Repro by Artilitho snc, Lavis-Trento, Italy.
www.artilitho.com
Printed/Bound by Offizin Andersen Nexö, Leipzig

ISBN 978-3-8003-4170-2

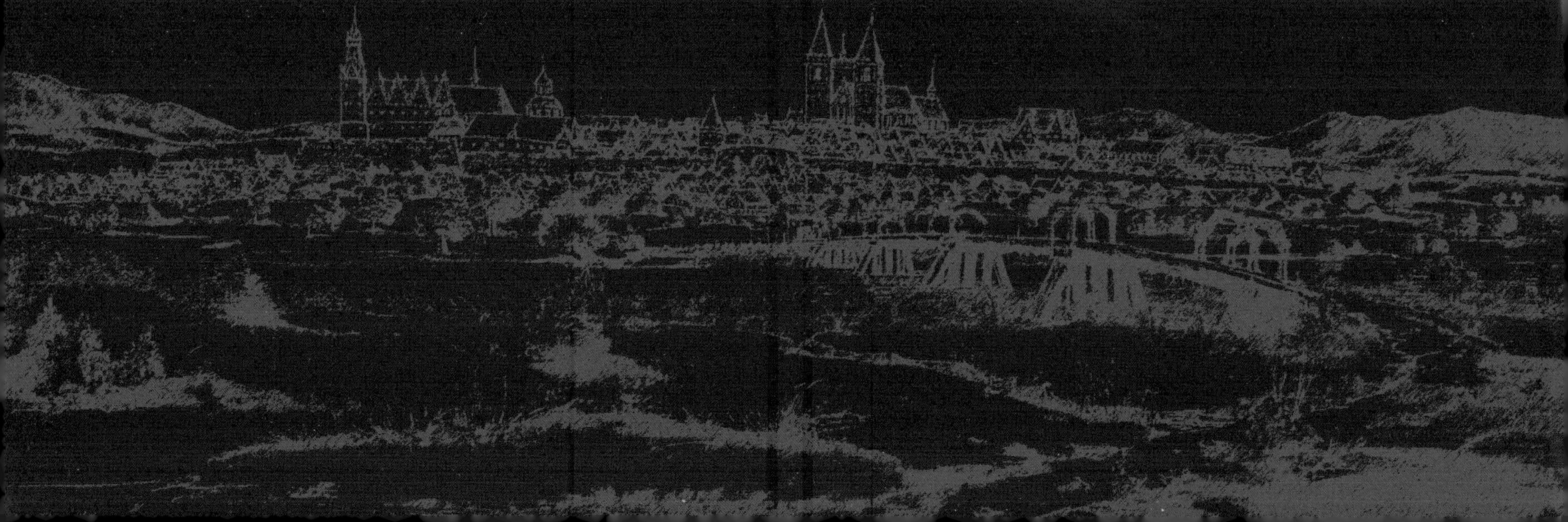